Love Notes From Dad

YOUR BREAKTHROUGH

Byron & Crystal Easterling

Build His House, Inc.
Camarillo, California

Copyright © 2018 by Byron & Crystal Easterling.

All rights reserved. No part of this publication may be reproduced, distributed or transmitted in any form or by any means, including photocopying, recording, or other electronic or mechanical methods, without the prior written permission of the publisher, except in the case of brief quotations embodied in critical reviews and certain other noncommercial uses permitted by copyright law. For permission requests, write to the publisher, addressed "Attention: Permissions Coordinator," at the address below.

Build His House, Inc
Camarillo, California 93010
www.PropheticWeekly.com

Book Layout ©2017 BookDesignTemplates.com

Ordering Information:
Quantity sales. Special discounts are available on quantity purchases by corporations, associations, and others. For details, contact BHHInternational@gmail.com

Love Notes From Dad/ Byron & Crystal Easterling. —1st ed.
ISBN 9781720266853

Contents

Echo My Voice 1
All Heaven Hears 9
Real Deal 17
A Promised Heart 25
Ready To Commune 37
Heart Beat 47
Your Footprint 57
I Think I'll Shout Your Name 69
Your Break Through 79
The Edge of Love 95
About The Authors 103

*Dedicated to Those Who
Love the Pursuit of the Father's Heart.*

Two years ago, I began writing what I called, Love Notes From Dad. They have become a part of our prophetic gatherings as we travel. They are simple expressions of how I believe the Father speaks of us and sees us from a heavenly point of view.

It was then that Crystal had the great idea to take these and create a daily devotional series. With five days for each Love Note. Allowing you to go deeper and hear the heartbeat of the Father for you through practical exercises, scripture, meditation and more. Crystal and I pray you will enjoy these moments with Dad and discover his abundant love for you as you search his heart through these Love Notes to you.

Byron

We are so thrilled to get to share these Love Notes from the Father with you. I know that I was touched as I read through them time after time. My heart for you is that you will be taken into a deeper place in the Father's heart, and that you will discover and experience more and more of His immense love for you.

The activations are designed to give you several paths of interacting with the Holy Spirit over at least a five-day period for each love note. This is so that you can spend more time digging into each one, mining for more of what the Father has for you in each love note, rather than moving on to a new thought the next day. Please take unhurried time with each activation to get the most out of it. The goal is not to "get it done', but to have a deep, joyful encounter and conversation with the Father each day. If you want to spend more time on a particular activation, please do so; take as much time as the Holy Spirit is leading you to.

Our prayer is that you will discover the height and width and depths of His love for you in ways you have never known before.

Crystal

Echo My Voice

*As you and I meet,
I promise that I will be in the middle of us
Connecting my Spirit with yours.
Causing our hearts to beat in rhythm,
And your voice to echo My voice.
What can happen amid My presence?
The options are limitless.
The opportunities endless!*

Day 1:

Take time to read and reread and meditate on this love note. Still your heart and mind, rest in His Presence. Journal your thoughts and meditations.

Stop to ponder the parts that stand out to you.
What is the Holy Spirit saying to you?

_____
_____
_____
_____
_____
_____
_____
_____
_____

Make a list of what the Holy Spirit is promising here.

_____
_____
_____
_____
_____
_____
_____
_____
_____
_____
_____
_____

How does your mind and heart respond to those promises?

_____
_____
_____
_____
_____
_____
_____
_____
_____

What emotions rise up in you?

_____
_____
_____
_____
_____
_____
_____
_____
_____

What do you desire from Him?

_____
_____
_____
_____
_____
_____
_____
_____

What possibilities and opportunities can you dream about as you meditate on these things?

Day 2:
Look at and meditate on these scriptures that speak to this love note. You can choose to stick on one, or several of them. Read and reread them. Read them out loud if you want. Let them soak into your spirit and mind. Then quiet your spirit and listen.

2Corinthians 6:16
1Corinthians 2:9-16
2Corinthians 13:14
Psalm 16:11
Psalm 27:4
John 17:21-30
1 John 5:14

What revelations did the Holy Spirit give you? Journal your thoughts and meditations.

___
___
___
___
___
___
___
___
___
___
___
___
___
___
___
___
___
___

Day 3:

Go deeper. Go back to your list of promises from Day 1 and the scriptures. Take His promises to heart and use this time to practice His Presence. Create an atmosphere He likes to come to! Quietly begin to worship and thank him for His promises. Enjoy His Presence. Breathe Him in. Soak in Him, don't be in a hurry. Go where He leads you.

What limitless possibilities can you imagine (1Cor. 2:9)? Ask Him to speak to you about what is on His heart. Journal what He shows to you and where He leads you. Begin to practice His Presence throughout your day(s).

_____
_____
_____
_____
_____
_____
_____
_____
_____
_____
_____
_____
_____
_____
_____
_____
_____
_____
_____

Practice His Presence as you are out and about in different situations by calling on His Name and quieting your spirit while thanking Him for His presence within you.

Day 4:

Write a prayer that declares the truths you received from the love note and the scriptures, and what the Holy Spirit has shown you from your meditations.

Declare these truths over yourself and thank Him for all that He is revealing to you. Pray them out loud over yourself daily until they become a normal part of your relationship with Him.

_____
_____
_____
_____
_____
_____
_____
_____
_____
_____
_____
_____
_____
_____
_____
_____
_____
_____
_____
_____
_____
_____
_____
_____
_____

Day 5:

Just spend some time in worship and praise today. Write a poem or prayer of praise and thanksgiving for what the Father has been revealing to you through this love note. Or express your heart through some other means of creative expression: draw or paint, dance, sing, anything you enjoy.

_____
_____
_____
_____
_____
_____
_____
_____
_____
_____
_____
_____
_____
_____
_____
_____
_____
_____
_____
_____
_____
_____
_____
_____

Share what you have been learning with someone else today.

All Heaven Hears

*I like calling you my child.
Do you know how proud I am of you?
Do you have any idea how much I speak about you?
You are on my lips day and night.
I think of you constantly.
You can't imagine this can you?
But I do – and all of heaven hears me!
When I think of you
I get the biggest smile.
You bring me great pleasure.*

Day 1:

Journal your thoughts regarding what is being said here. Write down whatever comes to your mind and heart.

_____
_____
_____
_____
_____
_____
_____
_____
_____
_____
_____
_____
_____
_____
_____
_____
_____
_____
_____
_____
_____
_____
_____
_____
_____
_____
_____
_____
_____
_____

Do you ever see yourself in this way, as His precious child? How do you believe the Father feels toward you?

___

Do you believe this? Is this how you relate to the Father?

___

Take time to meditate on these things today.

___

Day 2:

Look at and meditate on these scriptures that speak to this love note. You can choose to stick on one, or several of them. Read and reread them. Read them out loud. Let them soak into your spirit and mind. Quiet your spirit and listen. Just sit back and enjoy His Presence.

Psalm 139
Romans 8:34-35
Zephaniah 3:17
John 17:26
Ephesians 1:4-5

What is He speaking to your heart and mind? Journal what the Father speaks to you.

_____
_____
_____
_____
_____
_____
_____
_____
_____
_____
_____
_____
_____
_____
_____
_____
_____
_____
_____
_____

Day 3:

Go deeper. What false thoughts and beliefs about *yourself* need to change for you to come into agreement with what the Father has been showing you?

_____
_____
_____
_____
_____
_____
_____
_____
_____

What false thoughts and beliefs about the *Father's heart* towards you need to change to come into agreement with who He has said He is for you, and His heart towards you?

_____
_____
_____
_____
_____
_____
_____
_____
_____
_____
_____

Make a list of what He has said is true of Him, and who He has said you are to Him.

_____

_____
_____
_____
_____
_____
_____
_____
_____
_____
_____
_____
_____
_____
_____
_____
_____
_____
_____
_____
_____
_____
_____
_____
_____
_____
_____

Begin to put these truths into practice by rejecting the false and holding to what is true.

Day 4:

Write a prayer that declares the truths you have been learning from this love note over your life, using the scriptures and what the Father has shown you from your meditations.

_____
_____
_____
_____
_____
_____
_____
_____
_____
_____
_____
_____
_____
_____
_____
_____
_____
_____
_____
_____
_____
_____
_____
_____
_____

Declare these truths about his heart toward you each day until they become a part of you. Pray them out loud over yourself!

Day 5:

Spend some time in worship and praise today enjoying His Presence.

Write a poem or prayer of praise and thanksgiving for what the Father has been revealing to you through this love note. Or express your heart through some other means of creative expression: draw or paint, dance, sing, anything you enjoy.

_____
_____
_____
_____
_____
_____
_____
_____
_____
_____
_____
_____
_____
_____
_____
_____
_____
_____
_____
_____

Share what you have been learning with someone else today.

Real Deal

I never encounter you half way!
I am not a half way Father.
I didn't stumble onto our friendship.
I don't show up part way.
I'm a full out, full on, always there, ready to go – DAD!
I'm the real deal.
That's a great name – REAL DEAL.
You can call me Real Deal if you'd like.
No matter what you have seen before,
Whatever the distance of your earthly father,
The pain he may have caused you,
This. Is. Not. Me!
Never believe these lies!
I am with you always.
I never encounter you half way!
I am not a half way Father.
I didn't stumble onto our friendship.
I'm not a 100 percent Dad either.
I'm a 110 percenter!
I love that part of our relationship.
I remain more than 100 percent for you.

Today when you feel alone, even abandoned,
Maybe without hope or confused,
Longing for attention that no one seems able to satisfy
Remember...
I never encounter you half way!
I am not a half way Father.
I didn't stumble onto our friendship.
I'm your guy!
I'm the Real Deal,
A true 110 percenter!

Day 1:

Take time to read and reread this love note. Relax and enter His Presence.

Stop and meditate on the parts that catch your attention. Ask the Father questions you may have about it and listen for His answers.

Do you see the Father as ready, waiting, and eager for you to approach Him? Do you believe He will be there for you? How do you think this has affected your relationship with Him and how you spend time with Him? Journal your thoughts and impressions that you get from this love note.

_____
_____
_____
_____
_____
_____
_____
_____
_____
_____
_____
_____
_____
_____
_____
_____
_____
_____
_____
_____
_____
_____

Day 2:

As you sit in His Presence, look at and meditate on these scriptures that speak to this love note. You can choose to stick on one, or several of them. Read and reread them. Stop and ponder the parts that stick out to you. Read them out loud if you want. Let them soak into your spirit. Then quiet your spirit and listen. Afterwards, journal what the Father is speaking to you.

Romans 8:31-35
Romans 5:7-8
Romans 8:14-16
Psalms 103:4-14
Luke 12:7
2Corinthians 5:17
Philippians 3:13-14
Matthew 7:9-11

Day 3:

Go deeper. Scripture tells us we are transformed by the renewing of our mind.

Based on what the Father has been showing you, what ways of thinking and beliefs, about the way you relate to the Father, need to change to come into agreement with who He has said He is for you, and His heart towards you?

_____
_____
_____
_____
_____
_____
_____
_____
_____

Take some time to list and acknowledge what wrong thoughts you have entertained regarding the Father's heart and kind intentions towards you.

_____
_____
_____
_____
_____
_____
_____
_____
_____
_____

Compare those with the Truth of who He Says He is.

_____
_____
_____
_____
_____
_____
_____
_____
_____
_____
_____
_____
_____
_____
_____
_____
_____
_____

Now, as you sit in His Presence, ask The Father to give you a list of 5 things He says He wants to be for you. Relax and be patient. Write down whatever comes to your mind.

1. _____
2. _____
3. _____
4. _____
5. _____

Day 4:

Using what the Father has been showing you, write a prayer that declares the truths of His kindness and love for you. You can use the scriptures and what the Holy Spirit has spoken to you from your meditations.

_____
_____
_____
_____
_____
_____
_____
_____
_____
_____
_____
_____
_____
_____
_____
_____
_____
_____
_____
_____
_____
_____
_____
_____

Declare these truths about his heart toward you every day. Pray them out loud over yourself! And don't forget to thank Him.

Day 5:

Spend some time in worship and praise today, thanking Him for His great love for you.

Write a poem or prayer of praise and thanksgiving for what the Father has been revealing to you through this love note. Or express your heart through some other means of creative expression: draw or paint, dance, sing, anything you enjoy.

_____
_____
_____
_____
_____
_____
_____
_____
_____
_____
_____
_____
_____
_____
_____
_____
_____
_____
_____
_____
_____

Share what you have been learning with someone else today.

A Promised Heart

The enemy has been at your door,
Knocking and slamming the door.
The enemy is trying to break down the door!
What he doesn't realize is that he has been found out,
And he has been found wanting.
The attempts have been seen
And now it's time to stand.
To stand in the light of my power and truth.
Where can darkness hide when you stand in the midst of my light?
Is there a power or a presence able to bear its weight?
Who can outshine the light of my goodness,
Of my presence?
The enemy has been pounding on the door of your heart.
Your body has suffered the rage of pain,
Your heart has been afflicted with hope-deferred.
This was the goal of your opponent!
To crush and create a calloused heart;
To tire you of the battle.
Your opponent stands before God
Knowing his defeat.
The light of the Lord shines brightly,
Driving out – forcing back – vanquishing your foe!

Let the light of God's presence surround you!
Let your hope that was near death
Heal, strengthen and multiply.
Let my words become your words,
My heart become your heart.
For I am the way and the truth and the life.
I am the Father's pathway to his presence!
My life forfeited for you,
Once and for all.
Let hope arise and fill your heart and your mind.
Let hope overrun your family.
Let light cast fear into the darkness!
Let hope envelop your very home.
My power – My victory – My hope – My blessing!
To you, my child, I promise my heart and ever-increasing love.
For hope is built on nothing less
Than Jesus blood and righteousness!

Day 1:

Take your time to read and reread this love note. Let the words soak in and bring healing to you.

Journal your thoughts regarding what is being said. Write down whatever comes to your mind and heart. What portions stand out to you? Take time to stop and meditate on these.

_____
_____
_____
_____
_____
_____
_____
_____
_____
_____
_____
_____
_____
_____
_____
_____
_____
_____
_____
_____
_____
_____
_____
_____
_____

How have you dealt with difficulties in your life; now and in the past?

_____
_____
_____
_____
_____
_____
_____
_____

According to what is being said here, what does the Father make available for us during difficult times?

_____
_____
_____
_____
_____
_____
_____

As you sit in His Presence, let Him show you who He wants to be for you, and to do for you in these times.

_____
_____
_____
_____
_____
_____
_____
—

Day2:

Look at these scriptures that speak to this love note. What are these scriptures saying to you when you are going through difficulties?

Psalms; there are many to choose from here, but you may want to start with

Ps.3;18 ;27; or 91
Ephesians 6:10-18
Hebrews 4:16
and any others that
The Father calls to mind that
speak to your situation.

Journal what the Father is showing you.

_____
_____
_____
_____
_____
_____
_____
_____
_____
_____
_____
_____
_____
_____
_____
_____
_____
_____

As you sit with him in his Presence, take the time to read, reread, and meditate on the portions that catch your attention. What is He speaking to your heart?

_____
_____
_____
_____
_____
_____
_____

Is He offering you something that you need to pick up and act on?

_____
_____
_____
_____
_____
_____
_____

What do you need to take ahold of by faith?

_____
_____
_____
_____
_____
_____
_____
_____
_____

Day 3:

Go deeper. Read and meditate on the love note again. How have you typically dealt with difficult situations in your life?

_____
_____
_____
_____
_____
_____
_____
_____
_____

Have you held onto your belief and trust in the Father's heart towards you? Have you questioned His kind intentions towards you? Have you fallen for the enemies lies? What thoughts and beliefs are you holding on to that are contrary to what He has said or shown you about *himself* this week?

_____
_____
_____
_____
_____
_____
_____
_____
_____
_____

What thoughts do you need to replace with His truth?

_____
_____
_____
_____
_____
_____
_____
_____
_____
_____
_____

What language do you need to begin to use to speak words that agree with who He is for you?

_____
_____
_____
_____
_____
_____
_____
_____
_____
_____
_____
_____

How do your responses to difficult situations you have had in the past, or present, need to change in order for you to be able to take ahold of what He is making available instead?

_____
_____
_____
_____
_____
_____
_____
_____
_____
_____
_____

According to the love note, what kinds of things do you need to pick up and take a hold of instead?
Write out what "insteads" you need to put into practice.

_____
_____
_____
_____
_____
_____
_____
_____
_____
_____
_____
_____
_____

Day 4:

Write a prayer declaring His truth for your life from what He has been showing you. Include His promises toward you, with thanksgiving, for who He has said He is for you. Declare them out loud! Pick up your "sword" of Truth and chase the enemy down! Vanquish your foe by choosing to stand and rejoice in Him.

_____
_____
_____
_____
_____
_____
_____
_____
_____
_____
_____
_____
_____
_____
_____
_____
_____
_____
_____
_____
_____
_____
_____
_____
_____

Day 5:

Spend some time in worship and praise today. Thank Him for who He is for you.

Write a prayer or poem of praise and thanksgiving. Or express your heart through some other means of creative expression: draw or paint, dance, sing, or anything you like. Something that expresses your heart for what He has been showing you this week.

_____
_____
_____
_____
_____
_____
_____
_____
_____
_____
_____
_____
_____
_____
_____
_____
_____
_____
_____
_____

Share what He is giving you with someone else.

Ready To Commune

My desire is to have a heartfelt relationship with you.
To interact as a friend
Not as a judge.
I call us friends,
Intimate friends.
My desire is to open my heart to you,
That I might touch your heart
And connect at that intimate and vulnerable place.
How do I open my heart?
It's not a toil.
There is no insurmountable battle.
There is no mountain to climb.
It is a joy!
Open your heart to me,
To a loving Father
Who is always there,
Always present.

*My heart is open
And communion is never far away.
I have never been away,
Never forgotten you,
Or let you slip my mind.
I am not waiting like an angry teacher,
Waiting for their tardy pupil to finally arrive.
I am constantly sending you invitations
That I am here and ready to commune.*

*I am the best friend anyone can have!
The One who is here and expectant.*

Day 1:

Take time to read and reread this love note. Relax and enjoy His Presence. Stop and meditate on the parts that catch your attention. Journal your thoughts and meditations, and what He shows you.

How have you been approaching the Father?

_____
_____
_____
_____
_____
_____
_____
_____
_____
_____

How does this affect your relationship with Him?

_____
_____
_____
_____
_____
_____
_____
_____
_____
_____
_____
_____
_____
_____

Ask Him to show you how He would like to relate with you. How would this change your relationship with Him?

_____
_____
_____
_____
_____
_____
_____
_____
_____
_____
_____
_____
_____

What question(s) would you like to ask Him?

_____
_____
_____
_____
_____
_____
_____
_____
_____
_____
_____
_____
_____

Day 2:

As you sit in His Presence, look at and meditate on these scriptures that speak to this love note. You can choose to stick on one, or several of them. Read and reread them. Stop and ponder the parts that stick out to you. Read them out loud if you want. Let them soak into your spirit. Then quiet your spirit and listen.

John 17:3
John 17:22-26
John 15:15
John 16:13-15, 25-27
Hebrew s4:15-16
Hebrews 10:14-22
Luke 11:8-13
Psalm 139:1-10
Psalm 100:1-5

Journal what the Holy Spirit reveals to you.

_____
_____
_____
_____
_____
_____
_____
_____
_____
_____
_____
_____
_____
_____
_____
_____

Day 3:

Go deeper. Ponder and meditate on these things. Journal your answers to these questions.

How do you speak and interact with a close friend?

_____
_____
_____
_____
_____
_____
_____
_____
_____

A loving father?

_____
_____
_____
_____
_____
_____

What kind of relationship do you think He desires with you?

_____
_____
_____
_____
_____
_____

What have you believed about yourself, in how you have approached Him, that are contrary to His word, and heart and desire for you?

_____
_____
_____
_____
_____
_____
_____
_____

What have you believed about Him that is contrary to his heart, character and nature?

_____
_____
_____
_____
_____
_____
_____
_____

What changes in your approach to intimacy with the Father do you need to make to come into agreement with who He is saying He is for you?

_____
_____
_____
_____
_____
_____

What has He provided for you to come boldly into His Presence?

_____
_____
_____
_____
_____
_____
_____

What will you need to do differently in how you approach your intimacy with The Father?

_____
_____
_____
_____
_____
_____
_____
_____
_____

What do you need to start practicing?

_____
_____
_____
_____
_____
_____
_____
_____

Day 4:

Write a prayer that expresses your intimate heart response to the Father for what He has been showing you from the love note and the scriptures. Thank him specifically for how He has revealed Himself to you, and for His heart for you.

Ask Him to show you something about Himself as you pray. Take time to just listen; have a conversation with him about these things.

_____
_____
_____
_____
_____
_____
_____
_____
_____
_____
_____
_____
_____
_____
_____
_____
_____
_____
_____
_____
_____
_____

Day 5:

Spend some time in worship and praise today. Approach Him from a new place of intimacy.

Write a poem or prayer of praise and thanksgiving for what the Father has been revealing to you through this love note. Or express your heart to Him through some other means of creative expression: draw or paint, dance, sing, anything you enjoy.

_____
_____
_____
_____
_____
_____
_____
_____
_____
_____
_____
_____
_____
_____
_____
_____
_____
_____
_____
_____
_____
_____

Share what you have been learning with someone else today.

Heart Beat

You child are my heart beat.
Of all of creation
You have seized my heart.
You have undone my love.
Daily it intensifies for you.
Every time I gaze your way
I envisage the beauty
I have created in you.
It is a brilliant delight!

Day 1:

As you read and reread this love note, meditate on what is being said here. Take time to stop and ponder the parts that stand out to you. Journal the thoughts that the Holy Spirit speaks to your mind and heart.

How deep does the Father's love go?

_____
_____
_____
_____
_____
_____
_____
_____
_____

Are there limits to it? What does this make you think and feel about yourself?

_____
_____
_____
_____
_____
_____
_____
_____
_____
_____
_____

What does this say about the character and nature of God?

_____
_____
_____
_____
_____
_____
_____

Take time to meditate on these things today. Ask the Holy Spirit to speak to your heart about the Father's love for you. How does this change the way you relate to Him?

_____
_____
_____
_____
_____
_____
_____
_____

How would you like to relate to Him?

_____
_____
_____
_____
_____
_____
_____

Day 2:

Look at and meditate on these scriptures that speak to this love note. You can choose to stick on one, or several of them. Read and reread them. Read them out loud. Let them soak into your spirit.

Quiet your spirit and listen. Rest in Him and enjoy His Presence!
Psalms 139:1-18
Psalms 8
Isaiah 49:15-16
Ephesians 3:16-21
Song of Songs 2:10-14
Song of Songs 4:7-11
John 17:22-26

Journal what Holy Spirit is speaking to your heart and mind.

_____
_____
_____
_____
_____
_____
_____
_____
_____
_____
_____
_____
_____
_____
_____
_____
_____
_____
_____

Day 3:

Go deeper. Has He added to what He has already been showing you about how He sees you from other Love Notes?

_____
_____
_____
_____
_____
_____
_____
_____
_____
_____

Are you seeing a pattern? Is He wanting to get your attention on something?

_____
_____
_____
_____
_____
_____
_____
_____
_____
_____
_____
_____
_____
_____
_____

Do you think you value yourself the same way the Father does? Make a list of who He has said you are to Him from your reading and meditations.

_____
_____
_____
_____
_____
_____
_____
_____
_____
_____
_____

Ask the Father to show you 3 things He loves about you. Make a list of those things.
1. _____
2. _____
3. _____

What thoughts and beliefs about yourself need to change to come into agreement with who He has said you are to Him?

_____
_____
_____
_____
_____
_____
_____
_____
_____

How has the way you view the Father been changing?

_____
_____
_____
_____
_____
_____
_____
_____
_____
_____

Make a list of 3-character traits of the Father that are becoming more real in your experience of Him.
1. _____
2. _____
3. _____

In what ways that you have been relating to the Father, need change to come into agreement with who He has said He is for you, and His heart towards you?

_____
_____
_____
_____
_____
_____
_____
_____
_____
_____

In what new relational way can you approach Him today?

Day 4:

Write a prayer that declares the truths you have been learning from this love note over your life, using the scriptures and what the Holy Spirit has spoken to you from your meditations. Don't forget to thank Him for His love and kind intentions towards you.

Pray them out loud over yourself! Declare these truths about his heart toward you each day until they become a reality in your life.

_____
_____
_____
_____
_____
_____
_____
_____
_____
_____
_____
_____
_____
_____
_____
_____
_____
_____
_____
_____
_____
_____
_____
_____
_____

Day 5:

Spend some time in worship and praise today, thanking Him for His great love for you. Write a poem or prayer of praise and thanksgiving for what the Father has been revealing to you through this love note. Or express your heart through some other means of creative expression: draw or paint, dance, sing, anything you enjoy.

_____
_____
_____
_____
_____
_____
_____
_____
_____
_____
_____
_____
_____
_____
_____
_____
_____
_____
_____
_____
_____
_____
_____
_____

Share what you have been learning with someone else today.

Your Footprint

*Don't give up
What is rightfully yours!
If it doesn't stand against Me and my word
Then don't give it up.
I'm not trying to take things away,
I'm creating avenues for what I've placed in you!
Some call this pursuing your dreams,
Chasing your destiny.
The desires of your heart. (Ps 37:4)
No one can steal
What you hold on to!
Sometimes it's hard for you to continue believing.
Even when you don't,
I believe in you!
I know you!
I have created you to impact the world around you.*

To leave a footprint,
A lasting footprint.
Everyone leaves their footprint on the earth.
I am unfolding the impact of your footprint.
I believe in you!
I know you!
You should too.

Day 1:

As you read and reread this love note, take time to meditate on what is being said here. Stop and ponder the parts that stick out to you. Journal your thoughts about these things and what the Holy Spirit speaks to your mind and heart.

Has He put dreams and desires in your heart that you have questioned? It can be something very simple, or something very big, but it means something to you.

_____
_____
_____
_____
_____
_____
_____
_____
_____

What promises has he given you that you need to hold onto?

_____
_____
_____
_____
_____
_____
_____
_____
_____
_____
_____

Have you ever thought about the impact the Father has created you for? Take time to meditate on these things today. Ask the Holy Spirit to speak to you about the dreams and desires of your heart.

_____
_____
_____
_____
_____
_____
_____
_____
_____
_____
_____
_____
_____
_____
_____
_____
_____
_____
_____
_____
_____
_____
_____
_____
_____
_____
_____
_____
_____

Day 2:

Take time to look at and meditate on these scriptures that speak to this love note. You can choose to stick on one, or several of them. Read and reread them. Read them out loud. Let them soak into your spirit. Quiet your spirit and listen. Rest in Him and His Presence!

Psalm 37:1-6
2 Corinthians 1:20
John 1:3-5
John 15:15-16
Ephesians 2:4-10
Ephesians 3:10-21
Matthew 10:1
Hebrews 11
Matthew 5:13-16
Psalms 139:13-16

Journal what the Holy spirit shows you during your meditations.
_____
_____
_____
_____
_____
_____
_____
_____
_____
_____
_____
_____
_____
_____
_____
_____
_____
_____

Day 3:

Go deeper. Read and meditate on the love note again. Journal your thoughts on what that might look like.

What dreams and desires of your heart do you have? Write a sentence or two describing them.

_____
_____
_____
_____
_____
_____
_____
_____
_____
_____

Do you have promises connected with them, or other things? Write those out as well.

_____
_____
_____
_____
_____
_____
_____
_____
_____
_____
_____

Have you ever thought about the fact that the Father may have put those things within you? As you sit with the Father, ask the Holy Spirit to give you a picture of what he has put within you that He wants you to impact others with?

_____
_____
_____
_____
_____
_____
_____
_____
_____
_____

What changes in your thinking do you need to make to bring your faith into alignment with those promises?

_____
_____
_____
_____
_____
_____
_____
_____
_____
_____
_____
_____
_____

Can you picture yourself as that person in those dreams and promises? Are there practical things you can work on to become the person He has created you to be?

_____
_____
_____
_____
_____
_____
_____
_____
_____
_____
_____
_____
_____
_____
_____
_____
_____
_____
_____
_____
_____
_____
_____
_____
_____
_____
_____
_____

Day 4:

Do you have a promise? The enemy can't steal what you hold on to!

_____
_____
_____
_____
_____
_____
_____
_____
_____
_____
_____
_____

Since all His promises are "Yes and Amen" what can you do to activate your faith to hold onto those things?

_____
_____
_____
_____
_____
_____
_____
_____
_____
_____
_____
_____
_____
_____

Prayer is one way! Using what the Father has been showing you through this love note, or from previous things, write a prayer declaring the promises over your life and the impact He has created you to have.

Day 5:

Spend some time in worship and praise today. Thank Him for His wisdom in creating you.

Write a prayer or poem of praise and thanksgiving. Or express your heart through some other means of creative expression: draw or paint, dance, sing, or anything you like.

_____
_____
_____
_____
_____
_____
_____
_____
_____
_____
_____
_____
_____
_____
_____
_____
_____
_____
_____
_____
_____
_____

Share what He has been showing you with someone else.

I Think I'll Shout Your Name

I have seen you fight,
I have watched you battle;
You are a good warrior.
It is mans' way to stumble,
All men stumble.
I am not disappointed by what you call stumbling.
Do you know why?
You return to me.
You know my goodness.

So life is yours!
Hope is yours!
I call you:
Joy Bringer
Life Giver
Song Singer!
Fight on my friend
For I stand with you.
And who can stand against you
With me on your side!

I think I'll shout your name now!

Day 1:

Take time to read and reread this love note. Thank Him and rejoice in His love for you. Let the words soak into your spirit and mind. Stop and meditate on the parts that stand out to you.

Journal your thoughts regarding what is being said here. Write down whatever comes to your mind and heart.

What questions come to your mind and heart?

_____
_____
_____
_____
_____
_____
_____
_____
_____

What battles are you fighting?

_____
_____
_____
_____
_____
_____
_____
_____
_____
_____

How do you see yourself versus what the Father has made available for you to be in Him?

_____
_____
_____
_____
_____
_____
_____
_____
_____
_____
_____
_____
_____

How does it line up with what is being said here?

_____
_____
_____
_____
_____
_____
_____
_____
_____
_____
_____
_____
_____

Day 2:

Look at and meditate on these scriptures that speak to this love note. You can choose to stick on one, or several of them. Focus on the ones that stand out to you. Read and reread them. Read them out loud. Let them soak into your spirit and mind.

Make a list of the things these scriptures are saying is true of us as children of God. Journal your thoughts about the truths He is speaking to your spirit.

Romans 8:1
Romans 8:28-39
Ephesians 2:4-10
Revelations 2:17
Isaiah 62:2-5
Isaiah 61

Day 3:

Go deeper. Based on what the Father has been showing you, what ways of thinking and beliefs about the way you see yourself, need to change to come into agreement with who He has said you are?

_____
_____
_____
_____
_____
_____
_____
_____
_____
_____
_____

Take some time to list and acknowledge what false thoughts you have entertained regarding who you have believed yourself to be.

_____
_____
_____
_____
_____
_____
_____
_____
_____
_____
_____

Since we inherit the DNA of our Father, ask the Holy Spirit to show you 5 things He has made you to be in Him. Just relax, enjoy His Presence, and be patient. Write down whatever comes to your mind.

1. _____
2. _____
3. _____
4. _____
5. _____

Compare the way you have seen yourself with the Truth of who He has said you are.

_____
_____
_____
_____
_____
_____
_____
_____
_____
_____
_____
_____
_____
_____
_____
_____
_____
_____
_____
_____

Day 4:

Write a prayer that declares the truths you have received from the love note and the scriptures, and from the 5 things on your list from Day 3.

Write these as a statement beginning with the words, "I am…"

_____
_____
_____
_____
_____
_____
_____
_____
_____
_____
_____
_____
_____
_____
_____
_____
_____
_____
_____
_____
_____

Thank Him for His overcoming grace and the victorious life He has provided for you. Declare His truths about yourself and thank Him for all that He has given you in Christ. Pray them out loud over yourself daily until you begin to see yourself as He does!

Day 5:

Spend some time in worship and praise today. Is there a worship song that you know that expresses what He has been showing you?

Write a poem or prayer of praise and thanksgiving for what the Father has been revealing to you through this love note. Or express your heart through some other means of creative expression: draw or paint, dance, sing, anything you enjoy.

_____
_____
_____
_____
_____
_____
_____
_____
_____
_____
_____
_____
_____
_____
_____
_____
_____
_____
_____
_____
_____

Share what you have been learning with someone else today.

Your Break Through

Your prayers are sweet and beautiful to me;
They are tender and bring life.
Your heart is honorable and true
As you pour out good and sure words to me.
You have washed your heart in humility.
I hear.
Heaven hears
And is responding.
That path that was dark and covered with lies and deception
Is more than cleared away.
It is being prepared in beauty,
Fresh paths
In a lavish garden.
Thank you for partnering with me,
In preparation for your breakthrough.

Day 1:

As you read and reread this love note, take time to stop and meditate on what is being said here. Journal the thoughts the Holy Spirit speaks to your mind and heart.

What parts stand out to you?

_____
_____
_____
_____
_____
_____
_____
_____
_____
_____
_____

Ask the Holy Spirit questions about those.
What thoughts and emotions does this love note call forth in you?

_____
_____
_____
_____
_____
_____
_____
_____
_____
_____
_____
_____
_____

About your relationship with God?

___

What is your heart's desire in your relationship with Him?

___

How will this change the way you relate to Him?

___

How would you like to relate to Him?

Day 2:

Has He been awakening your heart and mind to an aspect of your relationship with Him that He wants to take to a deeper place?

_____
_____
_____
_____
_____
_____
_____
_____
_____

Are there lies and deceptions from your past, or from the enemy, regarding your relationship with the Father you been dealing with?

_____
_____
_____
_____
_____
_____
_____
_____
_____
_____
_____

What have you seen breakthrough in?

_____
_____
_____
_____
_____
_____
_____

What new ways of relating to Him has this opened for you?

_____
_____
_____
_____
_____
_____
_____

The words we speak and the thoughts we think will determine our mind's reality. What ways of thinking, and speaking, about your relationship with the Father needs to change in order to come into alignment with how He desires to relate to you?

_____
_____
_____
_____
_____
_____
_____

What words will you now choose to speak about your deepening relationship with Him?

_____
_____
_____
_____
_____
_____
_____
_____
_____
_____

As you sit quietly with Him, ask the Holy Spirit to show you 2 things that He wants to be for you now, that He wants to partner with you in. What are they?
1._____
2._____

In what new ways can you now relate to the Father in what He is making available to you?

_____
_____
_____
_____
_____
_____
_____
_____
_____
_____

How will you pursue these things with Him?

Day 3:

Go deeper. Where do you feel your relationship with the Father is now: acquaintance? close friend? intimate partner?

_____

Has He been awakening your heart and mind to an aspect of your relationship with Him that He wants to take to a deeper place?

_____
_____
_____
_____
_____
_____
_____
_____
_____
_____

Are there lies and deceptions from your past, or from the enemy, regarding your relationship with the Father you been dealing with?

_____
_____
_____
_____
_____
_____
_____
_____
_____
_____
_____

What have you seen breakthrough in?

_____
_____
_____
_____
_____
_____
_____
_____
_____

What new ways of relating to Him has this opened for you?

_____
_____
_____
_____
_____
_____
_____
_____
_____

The words we speak and the thoughts we think will determine our mind's reality. What ways of thinking, and speaking, about your relationship with the Father needs to change in order to come into alignment with how He desires to relate to you?

_____
_____
_____
_____
_____
_____
_____
_____
_____

What words will you now choose to speak about your deepening relationship with Him?

_____
_____
_____
_____
_____
_____
_____
_____
_____
_____

As you sit quietly with Him, ask the Holy Spirit to show you 2 things that He wants to be for you now, that He wants to partner with you in. What are they?

1._____
2._____

In what new ways can you now relate to the Father in what He is making available to you?

_____
_____
_____
_____
_____
_____
_____
_____
_____
_____
_____
_____

How will you pursue these things with Him?

Day 4:

Write a prayer that expresses your heart about your relationship with the Father, thanking Him for all that he is and wants to be for you.

_____
_____
_____
_____
_____
_____
_____
_____
_____
_____
_____
_____
_____
_____
_____
_____
_____
_____
_____
_____
_____
_____
_____
_____
_____
_____
_____
_____
_____

As you pray, ask Him for more revelation of His heart towards yourself and others. Journal what he speaks to you.

Day 5:

Spend some time in worship and praise today, thanking Him for His great love for you, and all that He has made available for you in Christ.

Write a poem or prayer of praise and thanksgiving for what the Father has been revealing to you through this love note. Or express your heart through some other means of creative expression: draw or paint, dance, sing, anything you enjoy.

_____

Share what you have been learning with someone else today.

The Edge of Love

*You are a great joy to me.
You long for me more than power,
More than glory.
You have turned your face towards me.
It brings laughter and rejoicing to my soul.
It rouses the heavens with my delight
When you say, "More, more of you God."
Thank you. The heavens celebrate you!
I love you more than you can ever understand.
To combine the love of your heart, your mind,
And your strength,
Is not the beginning of my love for you.
Gather all the people in one place,
Extend the greatest love mankind can summon
And it touches only the edge of my love for you.
For you!
You are why the cross was suffered.
You are why hell was endured.
You are My true love.
In this I will never change!*

Day 1:

What stands out to you here in this love note?

_____
_____
_____
_____
_____
_____
_____
_____
_____
_____
_____
_____

Still your thoughts and heart. Take time to read and reread and meditate on those things that catch your attention. What is the Holy Spirit saying to you?

_____
_____
_____
_____
_____
_____
_____
_____
_____
_____
_____
_____
_____

Can you imagine those in heaven rejoicing over you? Can you believe Jesus delights in you?

Ask Him to show you how He delights in you.

_____
_____
_____
_____
_____
_____
_____
_____

What thoughts does the Cross bring to your mind?

_____
_____
_____
_____
_____
_____
_____
_____

How does this affect you?

_____
_____
_____
_____
_____
_____
_____

Day2:

Look at and meditate on these scriptures that speak to this love note. You can choose to stick on one, or several of them. Read and reread them. Read them out loud. Let them soak into your spirit.
Quiet your spirit and listen. Just sit back and enjoy His Presence.

Zephaniah 3:14
Luke 15:7-10
1 Corinthians 2:9
Ephesians 2:4-7

Journal what Holy Spirit speaks to your heart and mind concerning His heart and thoughts towards you. What is He saying that is true about you?

_____
_____
_____
_____
_____
_____
_____
_____
_____
_____
_____
_____
_____
_____
_____
_____
_____
_____
_____
_____

Day 3:

Write a prayer that declares these truths over your life, using the scriptures and what the Holy Spirit has shown you from your meditations.

_____
_____
_____
_____
_____
_____
_____
_____
_____
_____
_____
_____
_____
_____
_____
_____
_____
_____
_____
_____
_____
_____
_____
_____
_____
_____
_____
_____

Declare these truths about his heart toward you each day. Pray them out loud over yourself!

Day 4:

Go deeper. Journal the thoughts and beliefs about yourself that need to change to come into agreement with what the Holy Spirit is showing you.

What thoughts and beliefs about The Father/God need to change to come into alignment with who He is saying He is for you, and His heart towards you?

_____
_____
_____
_____
_____
_____
_____
_____
_____
_____

Do you need to change the kind of language you use to speak about yourself or the Father's heart toward you? What is the new language you should use to describe yourself?

_____
_____
_____
_____
_____
_____
_____
_____
_____
_____

Write out these truths that Holy Spirit is showing you.

_____
_____
_____
_____
_____
_____
_____
_____
_____
_____
_____
_____
_____
_____
_____

How can you be intentional in putting these truths into practice?

_____
_____
_____
_____
_____
_____
_____
_____
_____
_____
_____
_____
_____
_____

Day 5:

Spend some time in worship and praise today. Put on some worship music if you like.

Write a poem or prayer of praise and thanksgiving for what the Father has been revealing to you through this love note. Or express your heart through some other means of creative expression: draw or paint, dance, sing, anything you enjoy.

_____
_____
_____
_____
_____
_____
_____
_____
_____
_____
_____
_____
_____
_____
_____
_____
_____
_____

Share what you have been learning with someone else today.

You may discover that in time this Love Note from Dad/The Edge of Love needs to be revisited. Use the 5 Days of interaction to step deeper into the heart storm of the Father's love for you.

About the Authors

Byron and Crystal Easterling are prophetic voices with heart's after the father. Their desire is to awaken every believer's identity in Christ Jesus and more fully empower them to deeply experience the Father's heart.

Byron and Crystal are founders of Build His House (BHH), a non-profit 501.c3 focused on creating excellent housing for widows and single mothers. The Easterling's serve on the boards of and advise several international ministries. Byron and Crystal have extensions of their work in many nations including Nicaragua. It is there that they helped to establish a farm program based from a prophecy he received in 2000 to help families break out of poverty and have a life sustaining income on a farm that they own.

In 2008, Byron authored, Dream Big Dream Often, and has since written well over 200 blogs based upon his spiritual journey, this new series, *Love Notes from Dad*, and they have an online prophetic community called PropheticWeekly.com.

Married in 1981, they have one married daughter, a fabulous son-in-law and a joyful granddaughter and fast-growing grandson. Byron & Crystal live in Camarillo, California.

To schedule an event contact BHH at BHHInternational@gmail.com

Made in the USA
San Bernardino, CA
17 January 2019